filipino

Designer: Benson Tan
Series Designer: Bernard Go Kwang Meng

This book contains previously published material from *Step-by-step Cooking: Filipino*

Copyright © 2013 Marshall Cavendish International (Asia) Private Limited

Published by Marshall Cavendish Cuisine
An imprint of Marshall Cavendish International

All rights reserved

No part of this publication may be reproduced, stored in a retrieval system or transmitted, in any form or by any means, electronic, mechanical, photocopying, recording or otherwise, without the prior permission of the copyright owner. Request for permission should be addressed to the Publisher, Marshall Cavendish International (Asia) Private Limited, 1 New Industrial Road, Singapore 536196. Tel: (65) 6213 9300, Fax: (65) 6285 4871.
E-mail: genref@sg.marshallcavendish.com   Online bookstore: www.marshallcavendish.com/genref

Limits of Liability/Disclaimer of Warranty: The Author and Publisher of this book have used their best efforts in preparing this book. The Publisher makes no representation or warranties with respect to the contents of this book and is not responsible for the outcome of any recipe in this book. While the Publisher has reviewed each recipe carefully, the reader may not always achieve the results desired due to variations in ingredients, cooking temperatures and individual cooking abilities. The Publisher shall in no event be liable for any loss of profit or any other commercial damage, including but not limited to special, incidental, consequential, or other damages.

Other Marshall Cavendish Offices:
Marshall Cavendish Corporation. 99 White Plains Road, Tarrytown NY 10591-9001, USA • Marshall Cavendish International (Thailand) Co Ltd. 253 Asoke, 12th Flr, Sukhumvit 21 Road, Klongtoey Nua, Wattana, Bangkok 10110, Thailand • Marshall Cavendish (Malaysia) Sdn Bhd, Times Subang, Lot 46, Subang Hi-Tech Industrial Park, Batu Tiga, 40000 Shah Alam, Selangor Darul Ehsan, Malaysia

Marshall Cavendish is a trademark of Times Publishing Limited

National Library Board Singapore Cataloguing in Publication Data

Diego, Arlene.
Filipino / Arlene Diego. -- Singapore : Marshall Cavendish Cuisine, c2013.
p. cm. – (Mini cookbooks)
ISBN : 978-981-4408-30-1 (pbk.)

1. Cooking, Philippine. I. Title.   II. Series: Mini cookbooks.

TX724.5
641.59599 -- dc23   OCN826278901

Printed in Singapore by Saik Wah Press Pte Ltd

contents

chicken broth with ginger and green papaya (tinola manok) 8

chicken and young coconut soup (chicken binakol) 10

macaroni soup (sopas) 13

beef shank broth (bulalo) 14

seafood chowder (sopa de mariscos) 16

taro leaves in spicy coconut milk (laing na gabi) 18

stewed vegetables with prawn paste (pinakbet tagalog) 20

raw fish salad (kinilaw na isda) 22

prawn and potato salad 24

fern fronds salad (ensaladang pako) 27

filipino-style spaghetti (spaghetti pilipino) 28

stir-fried noodles with spong e gourd and prawns
(ginisang patola at misua) 31

stir-fried egg noodles (pancit canton) 32

chicken porridge (arroz caldo con pollo) 34

filipino-style fried rice (sinangag) 37

chicken adobo (adobong manok) 38

chicken apritada (apritadang manok) 40

beef mechado (mechadong baka) 42

beef steak with onions and potatoes (bistek) 44

spanish beef roll (morcon) 46

filipino-style meat loaf (embutido) 50

beef stew (caldereta) 52

sweet and sour fish (escabeche) 54
prawn fritters with sweet and sour sauce
(camaron rebosado) 56
stewed vegetables with fish broth (dinendeng) 58
mexican stew with aubergine sauce (puchero) 60
fried stuffed squid (rellenong pusit) 62
grilled squid (inihaw na pusit) 64
young coconut pie (buko pie) 66
tri-coloured layer cake (sapin-sapin) 68
filipino créme caramel (leche flan) 70
corn pudding (maja blanca) 73
deep-fried spring rolls (lumpiang prito) 74
prawns in garlic sauce (gambas) 77
salted beef slices (tapa) 78
weights and measures 80

filipino

chicken broth with ginger and green papaya (tinola manok)

Flavoured with ginger, green papaya and drumstick leaves, Filipinos consider tinola as a one-pot meal. Serve it as a starter, on its own or a main dish accompanied with white rice.

INGREDIENTS

Cooking oil	60 ml (2 fl oz / ¼ cup)
Garlic	8 cloves, peeled and chopped
Onion	1, large, peeled and sliced
Young ginger	55 g (2 oz), peeled and thinly sliced
Fish sauce	60 ml (2 fl oz / ¼ cup)
Chicken	1, about 1 kg (2 lb 3 oz), cut into 12 pieces or bite-size pieces
Water	2 litres (64 fl oz / 8 cups)
Green papaya	1, medium, skinned, cut into half lengthwise and sliced into 2.5-cm (1-in) thick wedges
Salt	to taste
Drumstick leaves (*malunggay*)	to taste

NOTE
If green papaya is unavailable, substitute with chayote or vegetable pear (gourd).

METHOD

- In a saucepan, heat oil over medium heat. Fry garlic until golden brown. Add onion and fry until soft and translucent.

- Add ginger and fry until fragrant, then stir in fish sauce and mix well.

- Add chicken pieces and stir to mix well. Fry for 5 minutes, then add water and bring to the boil. Reduce to low heat, cover saucepan and leave mixture to simmer for 25 minutes. Add more water if necessary.

- Add papaya and increase heat. Bring soup to the boil and cook until papaya slices are tender. Add salt and drumstick leaves and stir to mix well.

- Dish out and serve immediately.

chicken and young coconut soup (chicken binakol)

An aromatic combination of young coconut, chicken and lemon grass, Chicken *Binakol* originates from the southern provinces of Luzon, where there is an abundance of coconut plantations.

INGREDIENTS

Cooking oil	60 ml (2 fl oz / 1/4 cup)
Garlic	5 cloves, peeled and crushed
Onion	1, large, peeled and chopped
Young ginger	2.5-cm (1-in) knob, peeled and sliced
Fish sauce	3 Tbsp
Lemon grass	3 stalks, bruised and cut into 5-cm (2-in) pieces
Whole chicken	about 1 kg (2 lb 3 oz), deboned and cut into bite-size pieces
Screwpine (pandan) leaves	2, knotted
Chicken stock	1.5 litres (48 fl oz / 6 cups)
Young coconut	1, flesh scooped out and juice reserved
Ground black pepper	1/2 tsp
Salt	to taste

NOTE

To open the coconut, use a cleaver to slice through the top of the coconut by making deep cuts gradually on one side in the same direction. After pouring out the coconut juice, use a spoon to scoop out the flesh. Discard any stray strands of fibrous husk.

For variation, medium-size prawns (shrimps) can be used instead of chicken, with the cooking time shortened by 10–15 minutes.

METHOD

- In a saucepan, heat oil over medium heat and fry garlic until golden brown. Add onion and fry until slightly translucent.

- Add ginger and fry until fragrant. Stir in fish sauce and mix well. Add lemon grass, chicken pieces and screwpine leaves and continue to fry for another 5 minutes.

- Add chicken stock and bring mixture to the boil. Reduce heat to low and leave to simmer for 25 minutes, or until chicken is cooked and tender.

- Add coconut flesh and stir in reserved coconut water. Season with pepper and salt and remove from heat.

- Ladle into serving bowls. Serve on its own as a starter, or as a main dish with rice and shallots if desired.

macaroni soup (sopas)

This well-loved Filipino comfort food is embued with the rich taste of chicken and milk, and the refreshing flavours of carrots and celery. In the Philippines, stock made from ham hock is used to give this soup a rich and smoky flavour.

INGREDIENTS

Cooking oil	60 ml (2 fl oz / 1/4 cup)
Garlic	2 cloves, peeled and finely chopped
Onion	1, large, peeled and minced
Chicken breast or fillet	200 g (7 oz), skin removed and cut into 2.5-cm (1-in) pieces
Carrot	60 g (2 oz), peeled and finely diced
Celery	30 g (1 oz), peeled and finely diced
Chicken stock or water	1.5 litres (48 fl oz / 6 cups)
Elbow macaroni	200 g (7 oz)
Milk	375 ml (12 fl oz / 1 1/2 cups)
Butter	40 g (1 1/4 oz)
Ground white pepper	1/2 tsp
Salt	to taste

NOTE
If making stock from ham hock, boil with 3 litres (96 fl oz / 12 1/2 cups) water, then reduce heat, cover and leave to simmer for 1 hour.

METHOD

- In a large saucepan, heat oil over medium heat. Fry garlic until light brown, then add onion and fry until soft.

- Add chicken, carrot and celery and stir-fry for 3 minutes. Add chicken stock or water and bring mixture to the boil.

- Add macaroni and cook for 8–10 minutes or until al dente. Reduce heat to low and add milk while stirring continuously. Add butter, then season with pepper and salt to taste. Leave mixture to simmer for 5–7 minutes or until soup is of desired consistency. Soup is ready to be served once chicken pieces change colour and macaroni and vegetables are tender.

- Dish out into serving bowls and serve immediately.

beef shank broth (bulalo)

Bulalo is a clear, tasty soup that derives its flavour from the bone marrow of beef shank. It originates from the Southern province of Batangas where cattle is raised and herded. Similar to Italy's *bollito misto* and France's *pot au feu*, it is a dish that is definitive of Filipino cuisine. The beef shank should be cooked until the meat, ligaments and tendons are almost gelatinous. For variety, add slices of cabbage and Chinese cabbage to turn it into a one-pot meal.

INGREDIENTS

Beef shank with bone marrow	about 2 kg (4 lb 6 oz), cut 8-cm (3-in) thick across the bone
Water	3 litres (96 fl oz / 12½ cups) or more
Fish sauce	60 ml (2 fl oz / ¼ cup), or to taste
Black peppercorns	1 Tbsp, coarsely crushed
Salt	to taste
Spring onions (scallions)	2, sliced

NOTE

If rushed for time, cooking *bulalo* in a pressure cooker reduces cooking time greatly. Simply place beef shank in a pressure cooker, add enough water to cover it completely and leave to cook for 30 minutes.

METHOD

- Place beef shank in a stock pot large enough to hold all ingredients. Add water to completely cover beef shank.

- Bring to the boil over high heat. Skim off any scum that rises to the surface. Reduce heat to low, cover pot and leave to simmer for 2 hours or until beef shank is tender and falls off easily from the bone.

- Season with fish sauce, black peppercorns and salt. Stir to mix well.

- Garnish with spring onions. Dish out and serve immediately.

seafood chowder (sopa de mariscos)

Also known as *bouillabaisse* or Fisherman's soup, *Sopa de Mariscos* is a medley of seafood that is simmered in a rich broth of tomatoes and fish stock. This is the Filipino adaptation of a Spanish recipe that is served on special occasions.

INGREDIENTS

Water	2 litres (64 fl oz / 8 cups)
Onions	2, large, peeled and sliced + 1, peeled and minced
Leeks	100 g (3½ oz), ends trimmed and finely sliced
Bay leaf	½
Clams	200 g (7 oz), scrubbed, then soaked in cold water for 30 minutes
Fish fillets	250 g (9 oz), sliced
Ground black pepper	1 tsp
Chicken or beef stock cube	½
Olive oil	60 ml (4 fl oz / ¼ cup)
Garlic	1 head, peeled and minced
Canned whole tomatoes	1 can, 440 g (16 oz), drain and chopped
Red capsicums (bell peppers)	125 g (4½ oz), cored, seeded and sliced into strips
Prawns (shrimps)	6, large, peeled and deveined, leaving tail intact
Squid	250 g (9 oz), sliced into 1-cm (½-in) thick rings
Sugar	2 Tbsp
Salt	to taste
Dried thyme	1 tsp

METHOD

- In a large pot, add water, sliced onions, leeks, bay leaf, clams, fish, pepper and chicken or beef stock cube. Bring mixture to the boil, then leave to simmer over medium heat for 15 minutes. Discard any clams that do not open. Remove from heat and set aside.

- Meanwhile, heat oil in a large saucepan over medium heat and fry garlic and minced onion until fragrant and onion is translucent. Add tomatoes and capsicums and stir to mix well.

- Add prawns, squid and broth mixture. Increase heat and bring to the boil, then reduce heat to medium and leave to simmer for 5 minutes.

- Season with sugar and salt and leave mixture to simmer for another 3 minutes.

- Sprinkle with thyme and remove from heat. Dish out and serve immediately.

taro leaves in spicy coconut milk (laing na gabi)

This spicy dish of taro leaves simmered in coconut milk comes from Bicol region in the southern part of Luzon, where coconut milk and chillies feature as main ingredients in the cuisine.

INGREDIENTS

Dried taro leaves	1 kg (2 lb 3 oz)
Fermented prawn (shrimp) paste (*bagoong alamang*)	100 g (3 1/2 oz) or use 45 g (1 1/2 oz) prawn (shrimp) paste (*belacan*)
Chicken thighs or drumsticks	300 g (10 oz), deboned and cut into 1-cm (1/2-in) cubes
Red chillies	85 g (3 oz), sliced diagonally
Green chillies	100 g (3 1/2 oz), sliced diagonally
Red bird's eye chillies	25 g (1 oz), sliced
Onions	2, medium, peeled and sliced
Garlic	5 cloves, peeled and finely chopped
Ginger	20 g (2/3 oz), peeled and sliced
Thick coconut milk	480 ml (16 1/5 fl oz) + 250 ml (8 fl oz) / 1 cup), mixed with 125 ml (4 fl oz / 1/2 cup) water into a smooth paste
Water	625 ml (20 fl oz / 2 1/2 cups)
Salt	to taste (optional)

NOTE

Fresh taro leaves may cause irritation to the throat. If used, they must be air or sun-dried until completely dry and wilted. This may take up to a week. Alternatively, use finely sliced fresh tapioca leaves.

METHOD

- Using your hands, shred taro leaves and discard hard stalks. Set aside.

- Heat a wok over medium heat and combine prawn paste, chicken, chillies, onions, garlic and ginger. Add taro leaves in batches at 1 minute intervals, allowing leaves to wilt and soften a little before adding the next batch. Stir to mix well. Add thick coconut milk and water and bring mixture to the boil.

- Reduce heat to medium low and leave to simmer for 10–15 minutes, or until taro leaves are soft and chicken is cooked. Stir mixture occasionally to prevent sticking. Add diluted coconut milk and simmer until oil starts to exude from mixture and liquid is almost completely evaporated. Add salt to taste if desired.

- Dish out and serve immediately with plain rice.

stewed vegetables with prawn paste (pinakbet tagalog)

This simple but nourishing dish originates from the Ilocos province in Northern Luzon. Flavoured with fermented prawns, *Pinakbet Tagalog* is popular all over the Philippines.

INGREDIENTS

Cooking oil	2 Tbsp
Garlic	5 cloves, peeled and crushed
Onion	1, medium, peeled and sliced
Fermented prawn (shrimp) paste (*bagoong alamang*)	55 g (2 oz) or use 30 g (1 oz) prawn (shrimp) paste (*belacan*), mixed with some water into a smooth paste
Tomato	1, medium, sliced
Chicken thighs or drumsticks	200 g (7 oz), deboned and cut into 1-cm ($1/2$-in) cubes
Prawns (shrimps)	150 g ($5^1/_3$ oz), small, peeled
Water	750 ml (24 fl oz / 3 cups)
Pumpkin	400 g ($14^1/_3$ oz), peeled and cut into 3-cm ($1^1/_2$-in) cubes
Aubergines (brinjals/ eggplants)	400 g ($14^1/_3$ oz), sliced on the diagonal into 1-cm ($1/2$-in) slices
Bitter gourds	400 g ($14^1/_3$ oz), seeded and sliced on the diagonal into 1-cm ($1/2$-in) thick slices
Ladies fingers (okra)	150 g ($5^1/_3$ oz), stems discarded
Salt	to taste

NOTE

Traditionally, *Pinakbet Tagalog* is not prepared in a wok, but in a pot where all ingredients are combined and cooked until the vegetables become "wrinkled", which is what *pinakbet* means.

METHOD

- In a large frying pan or wok, heat oil over medium heat. Fry garlic until light brown, then add onion and fry until soft.

- Add prawn paste and fry for 1 minute, then add tomato and fry for another 1 minute.

- Add chicken pieces and fry for 1 minute, then add prawns and stir to mix well. Cook until prawns turn pink and are cooked, then add water and bring to the boil.

- Add pumpkin and cover pan or wok. Reduce heat to low and leave mixture to simmer for 5 minutes, or until pumpkin is tender.

- Add aubergines, bitter gourds and ladies fingers and toss with ingredients to mix well. Cover and leave to simmer for another 5–7 minutes or until vegetables are tender. Stir occasionally to prevent burning. Season with salt if desired.

- Dish out and serve immediately with plain rice.

raw fish salad (kinilaw na isda)

A popular appetiser that goes well with ice-cold drinks and features at the table during special family occasions, kinilaw na isda is similar to the Latin American ceviche. This Visayan version features coconut milk that gives this dish a fuller, richer flavour. For maximum flavour, ensure each mouthful is made up of a little of every single ingredient.

INGREDIENTS

White fish fillets (mackerel, red snapper, yellow fin tuna or anchovy)	500 g (1 lb 1 1/2 oz)
Apple cider vinegar	125 ml (4 fl oz / 1/2 cup)
Calamansi or lemon juice	90 ml (3 fl oz / 3/8 cup)
Shallots	110 g (4 oz), peeled and thinly sliced
Young ginger	15 g (1/2 oz), peeled and thinly sliced
Tomato	1, medium, cut into 8 wedges
Red capsicum (bell pepper)	1, cored, seeded and sliced into strips
Coriander leaves (cilantro)	3 sprigs, finely chopped
Salt	to taste
Ground black pepper	1 tsp
Bird's eye chillies	3, sliced
Sugar	2 tsp
Thick coconut milk	85 ml (2 1/2 fl oz / 1/3 cup)
Red onion	1, large, peeled and finely sliced

NOTE

Use only fresh, saltwater fish with firm flesh, as softer fish will not be able to stand up to the acid in the vinegar. When marinating fish in vinegar, calamansi or lemon juice, avoid using a metal bowl as it may be corrosive.

METHOD

- Clean fish and remove all bones. Using a sharp knife, cut into bite-size pieces or strips.

- In a glass mixing bowl, place fish pieces and add vinegar. Leave aside to marinate for 30 minutes. Fish should have turned slightly opaque in colour after marination.

- Drain vinegar and add calamansi or lemon juice and mix well. Add remaining ingredients except for coconut milk and onion. Toss to mix well. Place in the refrigerator to chill for 2 hours.

- Just before serving, add coconut milk and stir to mix well.

- Transfer salad to a serving bowl and garnish with red onion. Serve immediately.

prawn and potato salad

The contrast of different textures, from the soft bite of potato to the crunchiness of water chestnuts, makes this an appetising and interesting salad.

INGREDIENTS

Prawns (shrimps)	500 g (1 lb 1½ oz), medium, peeled, leaving tails intact
Potatoes	1 kg (2 lb 3 oz), boiled, peeled and cut into 2.5-cm (1-in) cubes
Canned pineapple chunks	1 can, 500 g (1 lb 1½ oz), drained
Canned water chestnuts	1 can, 500 g (1 lb 1½ oz), drained and diced
Frozen green peas	200 g (7 oz), blanched and drained
Ground white pepper	2 tsp
Salt	2 tsp
Sugar	3 Tbsp

SALAD DRESSING

Mayonnaise	200 g (7 oz)
Double (heavy) cream	125 ml (4 fl oz / ½ cup)
Evaporated milk	125 ml (4 fl oz / ½ cup)

METHOD

- Bring a pot of salted water to the boil. Gently lower in prawns and leave to boil until they turn pink and are cooked. Drain and set aside to cool.

- Prepare salad dressing. In a bowl, combine mayonnaise, cream and milk and whisk until smooth. Set aside.

- In a mixing bowl, combine prawns, potatoes, pineapple, water chestnuts and peas. Add dressing, pepper, salt and sugar and toss to mix well. Place in the refrigerator to chill for at least 1 hour.

- Serve chilled.

fern fronds salad (ensaladang pako)

This unique Filipino salad features fiddlehead fern fronds, a local vegetable that grows in abundance in the woods and along the banks of streams in local villages. Use water convolvolus (*kang kong*) as a substitute if fern fronds are unavailable.

INGREDIENTS

Fiddlehead fern fronds (*pako*)	1 kg (2 lb 3 oz)
Fermented anchovies (*bagoong isda*)	85 g (3 oz), or use or fermented anchovy sauce (*budu*)
Tomatoes	200 g (7 oz), diced
Spanish onion	1, large, peeled and diced
Calamansi or lime juice	2 tsp

NOTE
If using fermented anchovies (*bagoong isda*), strain before using and remove any fish bones.

METHOD

- Choose tender young shoots and fronds that are firm and unblemished. Discard the hard part of the stems.

- Bring a pot of water to the boil and blanch ferns for 1 minute. Remove and place in a colander to drain thoroughly.

- Transfer ferns to a serving plate. Add remaining ingredients and toss well. Leave salad to cool to room temperature.

- Serve as an accompaniment to fried or grilled meat or fish, and plain rice.

filipino-style spaghetti (spaghetti pilipino)

This Filipino version is slightly sweeter than spaghetti Bolognese and is popularly served at children's parties.

INGREDIENTS

Olive oil	3 Tbsp
Garlic	5 cloves, peeled and chopped
Minced beef or chicken	500 g (1 lb 1½ oz)
Ground black pepper	1 tsp
Frankfurter sausages	400 g (14⅓ oz), diagonally sliced
Canned button mushrooms	255 g (6 oz), drained and sliced
Dried Italian herb mix	2 tsp
Tomato paste	140 g (5 oz)
Tomato purée or canned tomato sauce	900 g (2 lb)
Water	1.5 litres (48 fl oz / 6 cups)
Salt	3 Tbsp
Sugar	100 g (3½ oz)
Spaghetti	500 g (1 lb 1½ oz), cooked until al dente and kept warm
Grated Parmesan or Cheddar cheese	3 heaped Tbsp, or any desired amount for sprinkling

METHOD

- In a large saucepan, heat oil over medium heat. Fry garlic until fragrant, then add minced beef or chicken and pepper. Cook until meat is evenly browned., stirring constantly and using the spatula to break up any lumps.

- Add sliced sausages, mushrooms and dried herbs and fry for 3 minutes.

- Stir in tomato paste, tomato purée or sauce and water. Bring to the boil, then reduce heat to low and leave to simmer for 10 minutes. Stir occasionally to prevent burning. Season with salt and sugar. Taste and adjust seasoning, if necessary.

- Divide spaghetti among 3–4 individual serving plates. Remove sauce from heat and ladle over spaghetti. Sprinkle cheese over before serving.

stir-fried noodles with sponge gourd and prawns (ginisang patola at misua)

This is a popular noodle dish that is both delicious and easy to prepare. If sponge gourd is unavailable, substitute with other vegetables such as spinach, carrot, burdock, lotus root, broccoli or aubergine (brinjal/eggplant).

INGREDIENTS

Cooking oil	60 ml (2 fl oz / $1/4$ cup)
Garlic	5 cloves, peeled and crushed
Onion	1, medium, peeled and sliced
Fish sauce	2 Tbsp
Prawns (shrimps)	200 g (7 oz), peeled
Sponge gourd	500 g (1 lb $1^1/_2$ oz), ridges trimmed and sliced
Chicken stock or water	500 ml (16 fl oz / 2 cups)
Thin wheat noodles	200 g (7 oz)
Salt	to taste
Ground white pepper	to taste

METHOD

- In a frying pan, heat oil over medium heat. Fry garlic until light brown, then add onion and cook until soft and translucent.

- Add fish sauce and stir to mix well. Add prawns and cook until prawns turn pink and are cooked. Add sponge gourd and stock or water and bring mixture to the boil. Sponge gourd is cooked when soft.

- Add noodles and cook until noodles are tender. Season with salt and pepper.

- Dish out and serve immediately.

stir-fried egg noodles (pancit canton)

This is a popular Filipino-Chinese dish that is both tasty and filling.

INGREDIENTS

Cooking oil	85 ml (2½ fl oz / ⅓ cup)
Garlic	3 cloves, peeled and finely minced
Onion	1, medium, peeled and chopped
Chicken breasts or fillets	500 g (1 lb 1½ oz), cut into strips
Prawns (shrimps)	400 g (14⅓ oz), medium, peeled
Dried Chinese mushrooms	12, soaked to soften, stems discarded and sliced
Carrots	2, medium, cut into thin strips
Leeks	85 g (3 oz), thinly sliced
Snow peas	200 g (7 oz)
Cabbage	200 g (7 oz), sliced
Light soy sauce	60 ml (2 fl oz / ¼ cup)
Oyster sauce	60 ml (2 fl oz / ¼ cup)
Chicken stock	1 litre (32 fl oz / 4 cups)
Ground white pepper	1 tsp
Salt	to taste
Corn flour (cornstarch) (optional)	60 g (2 oz), mixed with 3 Tbsp water
Dried egg noodles	500 g (1 lb 1½ oz), soaked to soften for 2 minutes and drained
Calamansi limes	2, halved

METHOD

- In a wok, heat oil over medium heat. Fry garlic until light brown, then add onion and fry until soft and translucent. Increase heat, add chicken pieces and fry until lightly browned.

- Add prawns, mushrooms, carrots and leeks. Stir-fry for 3–5 minutes. Add snow peas and cabbage and stir to mix well. Add soy sauce, oyster sauce and chicken stock. Bring mixture to the boil, then reduce heat to low and leave to simmer for 3 minutes. Season with pepper and salt.

- If a thicker consistency for gravy is desired, stir in corn flour mixture and cook for 1 minute, stirring constantly. Gradually add noodles and gently toss to mix well. Stir-fry until noodles are tender.

- Dish out and serve immediately, with lime halves on the side.

chicken porridge (arroz caldo con pollo)

This simple, tasty dish of rice boiled in stock makes a nourishing meal.

INGREDIENTS

Cooking oil	3 Tbsp
Garlic	5 cloves, peeled and chopped
Onion	1, medium, peeled and chopped
Ginger	30 g (1 oz), peeled and finely sliced
Fish sauce	3 Tbsp
Chicken	1 kg (2 lb 3 oz), cut into pieces
Long-grain rice	375 g (12 oz), washed
Glutinous (sticky) rice	175 g (6 oz), washed
Rice-rinsing water or chicken stock	2 litres (64 fl oz / 8 cups)
Chicken stock cubes	2
Salt	to taste
Ground white pepper	to taste

CONDIMENTS

Chicken crackling	(see Method)
Spring onions (scallions)	2, chopped
Garlic	1 head, peeled, finely sliced and deep-fried until golden brown and crisp
Calamansi limes	2, halved
Fish sauce	
Hard-boiled eggs	2, peeled and halved

NOTE
Rice-rinsing water refers to the second or third rinse of water from washing rice before cooking.

METHOD

- In a medium-size pot, heat oil over high heat. Fry garlic until light brown, then add onion and ginger and fry for 2 minutes or until fragrant and onion is soft. Add fish sauce and chicken pieces and stir to mix well. Stir-fry for 5 minutes.

- Add both types of rice, rice-rinsing water or chicken stock and stock cubes. Bring mixture to the boil, then reduce heat to medium, cover pot and leave to cook for 1 hour or until rice is tender. Stir occasionally to prevent burning. If a smoother consistency is desired, leave to cook for 2–4 hours.

- To make chicken crackling, use 500 g (1 lb 1 1/2 oz) chicken skin. Wash and remove excess fats. Place chicken skin in a pot and cover with water. Add 1 tsp salt and bring to the boil. Reduce heat to medium and simmer until liquid is evaporated. Set chicken skin aside. Heat 500 ml (16 fl oz / 2 cups) oil in a wok over high heat. Deep-fry chicken skin until golden brown and crisp. Drain well and shred coarsely when cool.

- Season porridge with salt and pepper and leave to simmer for another 3 minutes before removing from heat. Dish out and serve immediately, with condiments on the side.

filipino-style fried rice (sinangag)

This simple dish of garlic fried rice is typically consumed on its own as a breakfast dish. However, it can be served up as a staple during a main meal with other dishes.

INGREDIENTS

Cooking oil	60 ml (2 fl oz / $1/4$ cup)
Garlic	1 head, peeled and minced
Cooked rice	1 kg (2 lb 3 oz), preferably refrigerated and chilled overnight
Salt	1 tsp
Tomatoes	2, chopped
Red onion	1, peeled and finely sliced

METHOD

- In a wok, heat oil over medium heat. Fry garlic until golden brown, then gradually add rice and salt. Toss rice to mix evenly and use your spatula to break up any lumps. Cook for 5 minutes or until heated through before removing from heat.

- Transfer rice to prepared serving plates and garnish with tomatoes and onion. Serve as part of a main meal with other dishes, or on its own.

chicken adobo (adobong manok)

Adobo is the national dish of the Philippines. It is usually made with chicken or pork, but other forms of poultry, such as quail, may also be used.

INGREDIENTS

Whole chicken	1, about 1.5 kg (3 lb 4 1/2 oz), cut into 12 serving pieces
Light soy sauce	60 ml (2 fl oz / 1/4 cup)
Apple cider vinegar or distilled vinegar	60 ml (2 fl oz / 1/4 cup)
Bay leaf	1, small
Garlic	1 head + 2 cloves, peeled and crushed
Black peppercorns	2–3 Tbsp
Water	500 ml (16 fl oz / 2 cups), or more if necessary
Cooking oil	90 ml (3 fl oz / 3/8 cup)
Sweet soy sauce	90 ml (3 fl oz / 3/8 cup)
Spanish onion	1, large, peeled and sliced
Salt	1–2 tsp

NOTE

Adobo is best served a day old, as its flavour intensifies over time. For a spicy variation, add 1 Tbsp chilli powder, or some chopped bird's eye chillies together with sweet soy sauce.

METHOD

- Place chicken pieces in a saucepan. Add light soy sauce, vinegar, bay leaf, 2 cloves crushed garlic, 2 Tbsp peppercorns and enough water to cover chicken.

- Bring mixture to the boil over high heat, then reduce heat to medium and leave to simmer, uncovered, until chicken is cooked and tender and liquid has reduced by half. Remove chicken pieces and set aside. Strain boiling liquid and reserve 375 ml (12 fl oz / 1 1/2 cups).

- In a large frying pan or wok, heat oil over medium heat. Fry remaining garlic until golden brown, then add chicken pieces and fry for 3 minutes or until light brown.

- Add sweet soy sauce and remaining peppercorns. Stir to mix well and stir-fry for 2 minutes.

- Add reserved boiling liquid and season with salt. Increase heat and bring to the boil, then reduce heat to medium and leave to simmer for 5 minutes. Add onion and stir to mix well. Leave for another 1–2 minutes to cook onion lightly.

- Remove from heat and transfer to a serving dish. Serve with Filipino-style Fried Rice (page 37).

chicken apritada (apritadang manok)

This is an easy dish of simmered chicken in a rich tomato sauce with fried potatoes and capsicum.

INGREDIENTS

Whole chicken	1, about 1.2 kg (2 lb 10 oz), cut into serving size pieces
Garlic	6 cloves, peeled and crushed
Distilled vinegar	60 ml (2 fl oz / $1/4$ cup)
Light soy sauce	60 ml (2 fl oz / $1/4$ cup)
Bay leaf	1, small
Ground black pepper	2 tsp
Water	1.25 litres (40 fl oz / 5 cups)
Cooking oil	60 ml (2 fl oz / $1/4$ cup)
Spanish onion	1, peeled and sliced
Sweet or light soy sauce	3 Tbsp
Ripe tomatoes	300 g ($10 1/2$ oz), seeded and chopped
Salt	to taste
Potatoes	500 g (1 lb $1 1/2$ oz), peeled, quartered and fried
Red capsicum (bell pepper)	1, small, cored, seeded and cut into 2.5-cm (1-in) cubes
Green peas	100 g ($3 1/2$ oz)

METHOD

- In a medium-sized saucepan, combine chicken pieces, 2 cloves garlic, vinegar, light soy sauce, bay leaf, $1/2$ tsp pepper and 750 ml (24 fl oz / 3 cups) water. Stir to mix well and bring to the boil over high heat, then reduce heat to medium and simmer, uncovered, for 12 minutes or until chicken pieces are tender. Remove chicken pieces, drain and set aside.

- In a large frying pan or wok, heat oil over medium heat. Fry chicken pieces until light brown, then remove and drain on absorbent paper. Reserve oil.

- Reheat reserved oil if necessary and fry remaining garlic until light brown. Add onion and cook until soft and translucent. Stir in sweet or light soy sauce and tomatoes. Mash tomatoes lightly with a spatula.

- Return chicken to the wok. Add potatoes and remaining water and bring to the boil. Reduce heat and simmer, uncovered for 12 minutes or until chicken is cooked.

- Season with salt and remaining pepper. Add capsicum and peas and cook for another 5 minutes before removing from heat.

- Dish out and serve immediately with plain rice.

beef mechado (mechadong baka)

Mechado is a Spanish dish that traditionally uses fatty cuts of beef. The addition of crushed biscuits gives the gravy a unique texture, and the fatty cuts of beef keeps the stew moist and flavourful.

INGREDIENTS

Stewing beef such as topside, brisket or chuck tender	1 kg (2 lb 3 oz), cut into 5-cm (2-in) cubes
Onion	1, large, peeled and quartered
Potatoes	5, medium, peeled and halved
Tomatoes	5, medium, finely diced
Red capsicum (bell pepper)	1, medium, cored, seeded and diced
Carrots	3, medium, peeled and cut into 7.5-cm (3-in) pieces
Light or sweet soy sauce	125 ml (4 fl oz / $\frac{1}{2}$ cup)
Salt	to taste
Ground black pepper	1 tsp
Water	1.5 litres (48 fl oz / 6 cups)
Digestive biscuits	100 g ($3\frac{1}{2}$ oz), crushed into semi-fine pieces

STOCK

Light soy sauce	60 ml (2 fl oz / $\frac{1}{4}$ cup)
Distilled vinegar	60 ml (2 fl oz / $\frac{1}{4}$ cup)
Bay leaf	1, small
Garlic	2 cloves, peeled and crushed
Ground black pepper	1 tsp
Water	2 litres (64 fl oz / 8 cups)

METHOD

- Prepare stock. In a pot, combine ingredients and add beef. Bring to the boil over high heat, then reduce heat to medium, cover pot and simmer until beef is tender.

- Remove beef and transfer to a clean saucepan. Strain stock and reserve 250 ml (8 fl oz / 1 cup).

- Add reserved stock and remaining ingredients to beef, except for crushed digestive biscuits. Bring to the boil over high heat, then reduce heat to medium and simmer for 10–15 minutes, or until potatoes are tender. Stir occasionally to prevent burning.

- Stir in crushed digestive biscuits. Taste and adjust seasoning, if necessary, stirring continuously until sauce has thickened.

- Dish out and serve immediately, with plain rice or crusty bread.

beef steak with onions and potatoes (bistek)

Simmered in a tangy marinade of soy sauce, lemon juice and pepper, bistek, a dish with Spanish and Mexican influences is considered to be one of the national dishes of the Philippines.

INGREDIENTS

Sweet soy sauce	90 ml (3 fl oz / ³/₈ cup)
Lemon juice	60 ml (2 fl oz / ¹/₄ cup)
Ground black pepper	¹/₂ tsp
Beef sirloin or tenderloin	500 g (1 lb 1¹/₂ oz), sliced into 7 x ¹/₂-cm (3 x ¹/₄-in) thick fillets
Water	375 ml (12 fl oz / 1¹/₂ cups), or more if necessary
Cooking oil	90 ml (3 fl oz / 3/8 cup)
Onions	2, large, peeled and sliced into rings
Light soy sauce	3 Tbsp
Potatoes	4, peeled and sliced into 4-cm (1¹/₂-in) thick wedges and fried until light brown
Salt	to taste
Corn flour (cornstarch)	2 tsp, mixed with 1 Tbsp water

METHOD

- In a mixing bowl, combine sweet soy sauce, lemon juice and pepper. Place beef slices in to steep and leave aside to marinate for at least 30 minutes. Reserve marinade.

- Transfer beef slices and marinade to a frying pan or wok. Add water and bring mixture to the boil over high heat. Reduce heat to medium and simmer, uncovered, for 10 minutes. Remove beef slices and set aside. Reserve liquid.

- In a clean frying pan, heat oil over medium heat and fry beef slices for 2 minutes. Add onions and light soy sauce and stir to mix well.

- Add fried potatoes and reserved liquid. Stir-fry for 3–5 minutes, or until potatoes are tender.

- Season with salt to taste and stir in cornflour mixture. Cook for 1 minute or until sauce thickens before removing from heat.

- Dish out and serve immediately with plain rice and salad greens if desired.

spanish beef roll (morcon) (Image on page 48)

Morcon is a dish that is associated with festive occasions because of its elaborate preparation. Once sliced, the myriad of colours from the stuffing gives the dish a festive appearance.

INGREDIENTS

Beef flank, skirt or round cut	2 kg (4 lb 6 oz)
Light soy sauce	125 ml (4 fl oz / $1/2$ cup)
Canned tomato sauce	125 ml (4 fl oz / $1/2$ cup)
Ground black pepper	1 tsp
Salt	1 tsp
Sugar	2 Tbsp

STUFFING

Carrots	2, peeled and sliced into $1/2$-cm ($1/4$-in) thick strips
Pickles (gherkins)	55 g (2 oz), sliced into thin strips
Red capsicum (bell pepper)	1, small, cored, seeded and sliced into thin strips
Any type of sausage such as chorizo	2, diagonally sliced
Hard-boiled eggs	9, peeled and halved
Plain (all-purpose) flour	for dusting
Cooking oil	90 ml (3 fl oz / $3/8$ cup)
Kitchen string	

BRAISING STOCK

Onion	1, large, peeled and quartered
Bay leaf	1, small
Sweet soy sauce	90 ml (3 fl oz / $3/8$ cup)
Canned tomato sauce	125 ml (4 fl oz / $1/2$ cup)
Sugar	2 Tbsp
Salt	1–2 tsp
Water	3 litres (96 fl oz / $12 1/2$ cups)

NOTE

Leave beef rolls to cool before slicing or it will not hold its shape.

MORCON SAUCE

Olive oil	2 Tbsp
Garlic	2 cloves, peeled and minced
Paprika	1 tsp
Reserved braising stock	
Salt and pepper	to taste

METHOD

- Butterfly beef. Place beef on a flat surface and use a sharp knife to cut through the middle without slicing through completely. Split beef open. Beginning on one side of beef, make diagonal, continuous 0.5-cm (1/4-in) cuts on beef. Repeat for other side of beef. Use a meat pounder to pound beef lightly to flatten, then slice beef into three 30 x 30-cm (12 x 12-in) pieces.

- In a large bowl, combine soy sauce, tomato sauce, pepper, salt and sugar. Place beef pieces in to steep and leave aside to marinate for 10 minutes.

- Place a piece of beef on a clean flat surface. On one end of beef, arrange one-third of stuffing ingredients except for eggs. Arrange carrots, pickles, capsicums and sausages side by side on top of beef so it creates a pretty pattern when rolled up. Place 3 eggs on top of ingredients, then roll beef up and tie with string to secure stuffing. Repeat step for remaining ingredients. Coat beef rolls with flour, dusting off any excess flour. In a frying pan, heat oil over medium heat and fry beef rolls until evenly browned.

- Transfer beef rolls to a large pot. Add braising stock ingredients and stir to mix well. Bring to the boil over high heat, then reduce heat to medium. Cover pot and simmer over low heat for 1 1/2 to 2 hours or until beef is tender. Remove beef rolls and set aside to cool. Discard string and reserve braising stock for morcon sauce.

- Prepare sauce. In a saucepan, heat oil over medium heat. Fry garlic until soft. Add paprika and pour in braising stock. Increase heat and bring to the boil, then reduce heat to low and simmer for 2 minutes, stirring continuously. Season with salt and pepper before removing from heat.

- When beef rolls have cooled, place on a serving platter and slice into 2.5-cm (1-in) slices. Serve as a main dish, with sauce on the side.

filipino-style meat loaf (embutido) (Image on page 49)

This dish can be served hot or cold depending on your preference. It can be prepared ahead of time and frozen, as it keeps well. It is usually served during festive occasions.

INGREDIENTS

Minced chicken or beef	500 g (1 lb 1½ oz)
Chorizo	3, chopped
Diced chicken or turkey ham	110 g (4 oz)
Red capsicum (bell pepper)	1, medium, cored, seeded and finely diced
Onion	1, large, peeled and finely diced
Celery	115 g (4 oz), finely diced
Carrot	1, finely diced
Pickles (gherkins)	55 g (2 oz)
Raisins	110 g (4 oz)
Grated Cheddar cheese	100 g (3½ oz)
Olives	85 g (3 oz), pitted and sliced
Bread slices	4, torn into small pieces
Eggs	3, lightly beaten
Salt	2 tsp
Ground black pepper	1 tsp
Hard-boiled eggs	5, peeled, ends cut off

BRAISING STOCK

Cooking oil	60 ml (2 fl oz / ½ cup)
Garlic	5 cloves, peeled and minced
Onion	1, medium, peeled and sliced
Tomato paste	55 g (2 oz)
Celery	1 stalk, roughly chopped
Water	2 litres (64 fl oz / 8 cups)

NOTE
Meat loaf is best sliced after it has been left to cool at room temperature before serving. If prepared ahead of time and frozen, omit hard-boiled eggs as they do not keep well.

MEAT LOAF SAUCE

Cooking oil	60 ml (2 fl oz / 1/4 cup)
Onion	1, medium, peeled and sliced
Plain (all-purpose) flour	60 g (2 oz)
Canned tomato sauce	45 ml (1 1/2 fl oz / 3 Tbsp)
Reserved stock	500 ml (16 fl oz / 2 cups)
Fresh milk	90 ml (3 fl oz / 3/8 cup)
Salt	to taste
Ground black pepper	to taste

METHOD

- In a mixing bowl, combine all ingredients except hard-boiled eggs. Mix well and divide into 2 equal portions. Place 1 portion of mixture in the middle of a 30 × 30-cm (12 × 12-in) sheet of aluminium foil, and spread mixture out into a 20 × 10-cm (8 × 4-in) rectangle.

- Arrange eggs on top in a row. Scoop remaining meat mixture over eggs. Fold up both sides of aluminium foil lengthwise and seal by tightly twisting together both ends of foil. Shape meat loaf by rolling it and twisting the ends of foil. Untwist the ends and fold in to seal. Set aside.

- Prepare braising stock. In a large pot, heat oil over medium heat. Fry garlic until fragrant. Add onion and fry until soft, then add tomato paste and celery. Add water and stir to mix well. Carefully lower meat loaf, still wrapped in foil, into braising stock and bring mixture to the boil. Reduce heat, cover pot and simmer for 45 minutes to 1 hour. Remove meat loaf and set aside to cool. Reserve braising stock.

- Place meat loaf on a roasting pan and unwrap one end of foil. Roast in a preheated oven at 180°C (350°F) for 25 minutes or until meat loaf is golden brown. Remove from heat and set aside to cool.

- Meanwhile, prepare meat loaf sauce. Heat oil in a saucepan over medium heat and fry onion until soft. Stir in flour and mix well. Add tomato sauce and reserved stock and increase heat. Bring to the boil, then reduce heat and leave to simmer for 3 minutes. Add milk, and season with salt and pepper. Leave to cook until sauce thickens.

- Place meat loaf on a serving platter and garnish with fresh herbs if desired. Serve warm or cold, with sauce on the side.

beef stew (caldereta)

Hot and spicy, *Caldereta* is embued with the rich flavour of beef, olives and tomato simmered in coconut milk and is commonly served at fiestas. Beef can also be substituted with lamb or mutton.

INGREDIENTS

SAUCE

Olive oil	60 ml (2 fl oz / 1/4 cup)
Margarine	40 g (1 1/4 oz)
Garlic	1 head, peeled and crushed
Onion	1, large, peeled and sliced
Tomato paste	55 g (2 oz)
Thick coconut milk	250 ml (8 fl oz / 1 cup)
Water	1 litre (32 fl oz / 4 cups)
Bird's eye chillies	12, crushed and chopped
Red capsicum (bell pepper)	1, medium, cored, seeded and quartered
Green olives	225 g (8 1/2 oz), pitted
Ground black pepper	1 tsp
Salt	to taste
Sugar	1 Tbsp

ATSUETE WATER

Water	60 ml (2 fl oz / 1/4 cup)
Annatto seeds	3 Tbsp

STOCK

Stewing beef such as brisket, ribs or mutton and lamb shoulder	1 kg (2 lb 3 oz), cut into 5-cm (2-in) cubes
Vinegar	60 ml (2 fl oz / 1/4 cup)
Light soy sauce	90 ml (3 fl oz 3/8 cup)
Garlic	2 cloves, peeled and crushed
Bay leaf	1
Ground black pepper	2 tsp
Water	3 litres (96 fl oz / 12 1/2 cups)

METHOD

- Prepare *atsuete* water. In a bowl, combine ingredients and stir to mix well. Using your hands, squeeze annatto seeds to extract as much red dye as possible. Strain and reserve liquid.

- Prepare stock. In a saucepan, place all ingredients and bring to the boil over high heat. Reduce heat to medium, cover pot and leave to simmer over medium heat for 1½ – 2 hours, or until beef is tender. Alternatively, use a pressure cooker and cook ingredients for 12–15 minutes. Remove beef pieces and reserve 250 ml (8 fl oz / 1 cup) stock.

- Prepare sauce. In a pot, heat oil and margarine over medium heat. Fry garlic until light brown, then add onion and fry until soft. Add beef and fry until evenly browned. Stir in *atsuete* water and tomato paste and mix well. Add reserved stock, coconut milk and water. Bring mixture to the boil, reduce heat and leave to simmer for 5 minutes. Add chillies, capsicum and olives. Season with pepper, salt and sugar. Simmer for another 5 minutes before removing from heat.

- Dish out and serve immediately with plain rice.

sweet and sour fish (escabeche)

Escabeche, which means "pickled" in Spanish, is a mixture of vinegar and spices used to marinate fresh or cooked fish and vegetables that are left to chill in the refrigerator overnight before serving. However, in the Philippines, *Escabeche* is a Chinese dish.

INGREDIENTS

Fish such as grouper, sea bass or perch	1, medium, about 600 g (1 lb 3 oz), cleaned, scaled and gutted
Salt	2½ tsp
Cooking oil	for deep-frying
Distilled vinegar	60 ml (4 fl oz / ¼ cup)
Sweet soy sauce	1 Tbsp
Sugar	85 g (3 oz)
Water	250 ml (8 fl oz / 1 cup)
Cooking oil	60 ml (2 fl oz / ¼ cup)
Garlic	5 cloves, peeled and finely chopped
Young ginger	15 g (½ oz), peeled and sliced into thin strips
Carrot	1, small, peeled and sliced into thin strips
Red capsicum (bell pepper)	1, small, cored, seeded and sliced into thin strips
Onion	1, large, peeled and sliced into rings
Corn flour (cornstarch)	1 Tbsp, mixed with 2 Tbsp water

METHOD

- Using a knife, score diagonal cuts on one side of fish. Season by rubbing 2 tsp salt all over fish and set aside.

- In a wok, heat oil for deep-frying over medium to high heat. Gently lower in fish and deep-fry for 7–10 minutes or until golden brown and crisp. Remove from heat and drain well. Place fish on a serving platter and set aside.

- In a mixing bowl, combine vinegar, soy sauce, sugar, water and remaining salt. Stir to mix well and set aside.

- In a frying pan, heat oil over medium heat. Fry garlic until light brown, then add ginger, carrot and capsicum and fry for 2 minutes. Add onion and fry until soft.

- Add vinegar mixture. Without stirring, increase heat and bring mixture to the boil. Reduce heat and stir in corn flour mixture. Leave to simmer for 2 minutes or until sauce thickens. Taste and adjust seasoning, if necessary. Remove from heat and spoon sauce over fish.

- Serve immediately.

prawn fritters with sweet and sour sauce (camaron rebosado)

This is a Filipino dish with a Spanish name, but with a Chinese style of preparation.

INGREDIENTS

Calamansi or lemon juice	2 tsp
Salt	1/2 tsp
Ground white pepper	1/2 tsp
Prawns (shrimps)	500 g (1 lb 1 1/2 oz), peeled and deveined, leaving tails intact
Cooking oil	for deep-frying

BATTER

Plain (all-purpose) flour	225 g (8 oz)
Corn flour (cornstarch)	110 g (4 oz)
Baking powder	1 tsp
Egg white	1
Ice water	180 ml (6 fl oz / 3/4 cup)

SAUCE

Cooking oil	60 ml (2 fl oz / 1/4 cup)
Onion	1, medium, peeled and quartered
Green capsicum (bell pepper)	1, small, cored, seeded and cut into strips
Red capsicum (bell pepper)	1, small, cored, seeded and cut into strips
Tomato ketchup	2 Tbsp
Oyster sauce	2 tsp
White vinegar	2 Tbsp
Sugar	55 g (2 oz)
Water	125 ml (4 fl oz / 1/2 cup)
Salt	1 tsp
Ground white pepper	1/2 tsp
Corn flour (cornstarch)	2 tsp, mixed with 3 Tbsp water

METHOD

- In a mixing bowl, combine calamansi or lemon juice, salt and pepper. Place prawns in to marinate and leave in the refrigerator until ready to use.

- Prepare batter. In a bowl, combine all ingredients and whisk until smooth. Place batter in the refrigerator to rest for at least 2 hours.

- In a wok, heat oil for deep-frying over medium to high heat. Coat prawns with batter, then deep-fry until golden brown and crisp, 5–6 pieces at a time, depending on how large the wok is. Do not put in too many prawns at the same time, as this will lower the oil's temperature and cause prawns to lose their crispness. Remove prawns from heat and drain on absorbent paper.

- Prepare sauce. In a saucepan, heat oil over medium heat. Fry onion and capsicum for 1 minute, then add remaining ingredients except for corn flour mixture. Increase heat and bring mixture to the boil. Stir in corn flour mixture and cook until sauce thickens. Remove from heat.

- Transfer prawns to a serving platter. Spoon sauce over or serve on the side. Serve immediately.

stewed vegetables with fish broth (dinendeng)

Dinendeng is a simpler and more affordable version of *Pinakbet* (page 20). Originating from Ilocos, it is a mixture of leftover fried fish and fresh local vegetables that is flavoured with fermented anchovies (*bagoong isda*). Fish sauce (*budu*) is used in this recipe as it is more readily available.

INGREDIENTS

Water	750 ml (24 fl oz / 3 cups)
Sweet potatoes	200 g (7 oz), peeled and cut 2.5-cm (1-in) cubes
Cherry tomatoes	100 g (3½ oz)
Onion	1, peeled and sliced
Fried or grilled fish such as catfish or Spanish mackerel	1, about 140 g (5 oz), cleaned, scaled and gutted
Fermented anchovy sauce (*budu*)	125 ml (4 fl oz / ½ cup) or use 90 ml (3 fl oz / ⅜ cup) fermented anchovies (*bagoong isda*) if available
Aubergines (brinjals/eggplants)	10, large, stems removed and quartered
Bitter gourds	4, small, halved, white pith removed and seeded
Salt	to taste (optional)

NOTE
As compared to fermented anchovy sauce (*budu*), fermented anchovies (*bagoong isda*) are more salty and pungent. If using, strain before adding to ingredients to remove any fish bones.

METHOD

- In a pot, add water, sweet potatoes, tomatoes, onion, fish and anchovy sauce or fermented anchovies. Bring mixture to the boil over medium heat for 5 minutes, or until sweet potatoes are tender.

- Add aubergines and bitter gourds. Reduce heat to low, cover pot and leave to cook for 10 minutes, or until vegetables are tender. Season with salt if desired.

- Dish out and serve immediately with plain rice.

mexican stew with aubergine sauce (puchero

Puchero is considered to be a one pot-meal. It is Spanish in origin and is normally cooked with beef and chicken, but fish makes a delicious substitute.

INGREDIENTS

Cooking oil	for deep-frying
Fish such as grouper, sea bass, perch or snake head	1 kg (2 lb 3 oz) cleaned, scaled, gutted and diagonally sliced into steaks
Baby potatoes	3, peeled, quartered and fried until light brown
Plantain bananas	2, about 200 g (7 oz), peeled and sliced on the diagonal
Cooking oil	90 ml (3 fl oz / 3/8 cup)
Garlic	2 cloves, peeled and chopped
Onion	1, large, peeled and sliced
Tomatoes	500 g (1 lb 1 1/2 oz), diced
Water	1 litre (32 fl oz / 4 cups)
Salt	2 tsp or to taste
Ground white pepper	1 tsp
Chorizo or any spicy sausage	200 g (7 oz), sliced on the diagonal into 2.5-cm (1-in) pieces
Cabbage	1, small, cored and quartered into wedges
Chinese cabbage	200 g (7 oz)
Canned chickpeas	200 g (7 oz), drained
Milk	90 ml (3 fl oz / 3/8 cup)

AUBERGINE SAUCE

Aubergines (brinjals / eggplants)	2, medium
Vinegar	60 ml (2 fl oz / 1/4 cup)
Garlic	2 cloves, peeled and minced
Salt	to taste
Ground black pepper	to taste
Sugar	1 Tbsp

METHOD

- Prepare aubergine sauce. Grill aubergines for 15–20 minutes on each side until skin is charred. Remove from heat and set aside to cool. Peel aubergines and discard skin. Place in a mixing bowl, add remaining ingredients and mash to combine. Set aside.

- In a wok, heat oil for deep-frying over medium to high heat. Deep-fry fish for 3 minutes on each side or until half-cooked. Remove from heat, drain and set aside. Reserve 90 ml (3 fl oz / $^3/_8$ cup) oil.

- In a saucepan, heat reserved oil over medium heat. Fry potatoes until golden brown. Remove from heat, drain and set aside. Using the same saucepan, fry bananas over medium heat until light brown. Remove from heat, drain and set aside.

- In a clean wok, heat oil over medium heat. Fry garlic until golden brown. Add onion and fry until soft and translucent. Add tomatoes and cook for 3 minutes. Add water and stir to mix well. Increase heat and bring mixture to the boil. Add fried potatoes and reduce heat to medium. Leave to simmer for 5 minutes and season with salt and pepper.

- Add fish, bananas and remaining ingredients and return mixture to the boil. Leave to simmer for 5 minutes or until vegetables are tender.

- Dish out and serve immediately, with aubergine sauce and plain rice on the side.

fried stuffed squid (rellenong pusit)

This hearty seafood dish is simple and easy to prepare. Feel free to experiment with different ingredients for the stuffing!

INGREDIENTS

Large squid	1 kg (2 lb 3 oz)
Calamansi juice	2 tsp
Light soy sauce	60 ml (2 fl oz / $^1/_4$ cup)
Salt	to taste
Ground black pepper	to taste
Cooking oil	for deep-frying

STUFFING

Cooking oil	60 ml (2 fl oz / $^1/_4$ cup)
Garlic	2 cloves, peeled and chopped
Spanish onion	1, peeled and diced
Fish sauce	1 Tbsp
Minced chicken	300 g ($10^1/_2$ oz)
Carrot	1, small, diced
Red capsicums (bell pepper)	30 g (1 oz), cored, seeded and diced
Peas	70 g ($2^1/_2$ oz)
Salt	to taste
Ground black pepper	$^1/_2$ tsp
Sugar	1 tsp
Plain (all-purpose) flour	for coating

METHOD

- Clean squid. Separate squid heads from tubes and set aside. Remove innards and ink sac, then peel away as much skin as possible. Rinse well and set aside.

- In a mixing bowl, combine calamansi juice, soy sauce, salt and pepper. Place squid in and marinate for 30 minutes.

- Prepare stuffing. In a frying pan, heat oil over medium heat. Fry garlic until golden brown, then add onion and fry until soft and translucent. Add fish sauce and minced chicken and stir-fry until chicken is well cooked. Add carrot, capsicums and peas and stir-fry for 2 minutes or until tender. Season with salt, pepper and sugar and stir to mix well. Remove from heat and set aside to cool.

- Fill squid tubes with stuffing until almost full, then stuff heads in and secure with toothpicks. Coat squid in flour just before deep-frying.

- In a wok, heat oil for deep-frying over medium heat. Fry squids until light brown and tender. Remove from heat and drain well.

- Slice squid into 3-cm (1½-in) rings and serve immediately.

grilled squid (inihaw na pusit)

This dish of tenderly grilled squid marinated in a combination of tangy, salty flavours is tasty and filling without being overly oily.

INGREDIENTS

Large squid	10
Lemon juice	1 Tbsp
Light soy sauce	85 ml (2^1/$_2$ fl oz / ^{1}/$_3$ cup)
Salt	1 tsp
Ground white pepper	1^1/$_2$ tsp
Tomatoes	2, large, diced
Spanish onions	2, medium, peeled and diced
Cooking oil	1 Tbsp

GARLIC-VINEGAR DIP

Distilled vinegar	125 ml (4 fl oz / ^{1}/$_2$ cup)
Water	60 ml (2 fl oz / ^{1}/$_4$ cup)
Garlic	4 cloves, peeled and crushed
Salt	^{1}/$_2$ tsp
Ground white pepper	1/4 tsp
Sugar	1 Tbsp
Red and green bird's eye chillies	3, crushed

METHOD

- Prepare garlic-vinegar dip. In a saucepan, combine vinegar and water over medium heat. Without stirring, bring mixture to the boil for a few seconds. Remove from heat and set aside to cool completely. Add remaining ingredients and set aside.

- Clean squid (page 63). In a mixing bowl, combine lemon juice, soy sauce, ^{1}/$_2$ tsp salt and 1 tsp pepper. Place squid in to steep and leave aside to marinate for 30 minutes. Reserve marinade.

- Meanwhile, in a bowl, combine tomatoes, onions, remaining salt and pepper and mix well.

- Fill squid tubes with tomato mixture until almost full, then stuff heads in and secure with toothpicks. Lightly brush squids with oil, then score several cuts on one side of tubes.

- Lightly grease a frying pan or grill pan. In several batches, grill squid for about 3–5 minutes on each side over medium to high heat, until squid is tender and lightly charred. Lightly brush with reserved marinade while grilling.

- Serve immediately with garlic-vinegar dip on the side.

young coconut pie (buko pie)

Here, a rich, buttery pastry encases a sweet, creamy filling made from young coconut (*buko*). Serve as a dessert or tea-time snack with coffee.

INGREDIENTS

Young coconut	1, about 450 g (16 oz)
Milk	250 ml (8 fl oz / 1 cup)
Single (light) cream	300 ml (10 fl oz / 1¼ cups)
Sugar	85 g (3 oz)
Egg yolks	5
Plain (all-purpose) flour	60 g (2 oz)
Vanilla essence	1 tsp
Screwpine (pandan) leaves	3, knotted
Egg wash	1 egg yolk mixed with 1 Tbsp fresh milk

PASTRY

Plain (all-purpose) flour	280 g (10 oz)
Sugar	3 Tbsp
Salt	½ tsp
Vegetable shortening	70 g (2½ oz)
Butter	85 g (3 oz), cubed
Egg	1
Ice water	60 ml (2 fl oz / ¼ cup)

METHOD

- Prepare pastry. In a mixing bowl, combine flour, sugar and salt. Cut in shortening and butter with pastry cutter until mixture resembles coarse meal.

- Crack egg into mixture and stir lightly to combine. Gradually add water and using a fork, mix until dough starts to come together. Using your fingertips, knead dough until smooth. Roll into a ball, cover with plastic wrap and refrigerate for 30 minutes.

- Meanwhile, pour water from coconut into a bowl and scrape out flesh (page 10).

- In a saucepan, combine coconut water, milk, cream, sugar, egg yolks, flour, vanilla essence and screwpine leaves over medium heat, stirring constantly until mixture thickens. Remove from heat and set aside to cool. Add coconut flesh, mix well and set aside.

- Preheat oven to 200°C (400°F). Divide dough into 2 parts, one three times bigger than the other. Roll out bigger portion to line a 23-cm (9-in) pie dish. Using a fork, prick base and sides of dough. Bake for 20 minutes or until pastry is light brown. Remove from heat and keep oven heated. Pour in coconut mixture, spreading evenly.

- Roll out remaining dough into a 24-cm (9 1/2-in) long sheet. Cut into a 1-cm (1/2-in) wide strips and place over filling, creating a lattice design if desired. Lightly brush with egg wash, then return pie to oven to bake for 25 minutes or until golden brown.

- Serve warm.

tri-coloured layer cake (sapin-sapin)

literally translated as "on top of the other", *Sapin-sapin* is a dessert made of glutinous rice flour. Colourful and attractive, this dessert is guaranteed to be a hit at parties!

INGREDIENTS

Glutinous (sticky) rice flour	200 g (7 oz)
Rice flour	170 g (6 oz)
Thick coconut milk	1 litre (32 fl oz / 4 cups)
Sweetened condensed milk	300 ml (10 fl oz / 1 1/4 cups)
Yellow food colouring	1 tsp
Jack fruit finely diced	125 g (4 1/2 oz), peeled and
Yam (*ube*)	500 g (1 lb 1 1/2 oz), peeled, boiled until soft and mashed
Purple food colouring	1 tsp

COCONUT MILK NUGGETS (LATIK)
Thick coconut milk   500 ml (16 fl oz / 2 cups)

METHOD

- Prepare coconut milk nuggets. In a wok, heat coconut milk over medium heat and bring to the boil. Reduce heat to low and leave to simmer, stirring occasionally to prevent burning, until oil separates and coconut milk starts to curdle and solidify. Continue cooking until nuggets are golden brown. Remove from heat and strain. Set aside and reserve oil.

- Line a 25-cm (10-in) round cake pan with aluminium foil. Lightly grease foil with reserved oil. Set aside.

- In a mixing bowl, combine flours, coconut milk and condensed milk. Whisk until mixture is smooth. Strain to remove lumps. Divide mixture into 3 equal portions.

- To one portion of flour, add yellow food colouring and jackfruit, then stir to mix well. To the other portion, add mashed yam and purple food colouring, then stir to mix well.

- Pour jackfruit mixture into prepared pan. Steam mixture for 25–30 minutes or until firm to the touch. Pour over yam mixture and steam for another 25–30 minutes or until firm to the touch. Pour in remaining coconut mixture and steam for another 25–30 minutes or until firm to the touch. Remove from heat and flip it out of the pan onto a serving dish. Set aside to cool for 30 minutes.

- Sprinkle coconut milk nuggets on top of layer cake before serving.

filipino créme caramel (leche flan)

There are many versions of this Filipino dessert, which is practically a staple at tea-time and festive gatherings. This is a classic version that features the distinct flavour and aroma of lemon and vanilla.

INGREDIENTS

Sugar	170 g (6 oz)
Water	90 ml (3 fl oz / $^3/_8$ cup)

CUSTARD

Eggs	5
Egg yolks	15
Sweetened condensed milk	450 ml (15 fl oz / $1^3/_4$ cups)
Milk	450 ml (15 fl oz / $1^3/_4$ cups)
Water	450 ml (15 fl oz / $1^3/_4$ cups)
Vanilla essence	1 tsp
Lemon or lime zest	2 tsp

NOTE
Filipino créme caramel is traditionally made with duck eggs for a better texture, flavour and colour.

METHOD

- In a saucepan, melt sugar over low heat, stirring constantly with a wooden spoon until melted and dark brown. Add water and increase heat to medium. Stir until sugar dissolves completely. Remove from heat and pour syrup into a 27-cm ($10^1/_2$-in) flan mould. Set aside for caramel to cool completely.

- Preheat oven to 190°C (375°F).

- Crack eggs into a mixing bowl and add egg yolks and condensed milk. Whisk until well blended. Add milk, water and vanilla and whisk lightly until just combined. Strain and pour on top of cooled caramel syrup, then stir in lemon or lime zest. Cover and seal with aluminium foil.

- Place mould on a deep baking tray and fill tray with water until it reaches 1-cm ($^1/_2$-in) up the sides of mould. Bake for $1^3/_4$–2 hours, or until créme caramel is firm to the touch. Remove from heat and discard aluminium foil. Set aside to cool completely before placing in the refrigerator to chill for 1 hour.

- To unmould, run a sharp knife along the edges of créme caramel. Place a serving plate on top of mould and invert mould. Gently remove mould and ease créme caramel out.

- Garnish as desired. Serve chilled.

corn pudding (maja blanca)

Originating from Pampanga, a district in the Central Luzon region, *Maja Blanca*, or *Tibok-tibok* as it is known there, is a sweet corn pudding traditionally made with carabao milk.

INGREDIENTS

Coconut milk nuggets (page 68)	1 recipe
Wilted banana leaf	1, large
Thick coconut milk	1 litre (32 fl oz / 4 cups)
Corn flour (cornstarch)	115 g ($4^1/_5$ oz)
Sugar	180 g (6 oz)
Canned creamed corn	125 g ($4^1/_2$ oz)
Ripe jack fruit	85 g (3 oz), finely chopped
Butter	125 g ($4^1/_2$ oz), melted
Yellow food colouring	$^1/_4$ tsp

METHOD

- Prepare coconut milk nuggets (page 68). Reserve oil and set aside.

- Prepare a 18 x 27-cm (7 x $10^1/_2$-in) rectangular pan. Trim banana leaf to fit and line pan. Lightly grease leaf with reserve coconut oil.

- In a medium bowl, combine 360 ml (12 fl oz / $1^1/_2$ cups) coconut milk and corn flour and whisk until smooth. Set aside.

- In a wok or frying pan, combine remaining coconut milk and sugar and bring to the boil over medium heat. Add coconut milk and corn flour mixture and stir continuously with a whisk until smooth and lightly thickened.

- Add creamed corn, jack fruit, butter and food colouring and cook until mixture has a firm, thick consistency. Remove from heat, pour into prepared pan and level with a palette knife or spatula. Set aside to cool completely before refrigerating for 1 hour.

- Slice pudding and sprinkle with coconut milk nuggets. Serve chilled or at room temperature.

deep-fried spring rolls (lumpiang prito)

Piping hot spring rolls are favoured as a *mirienda*, or snack, in the Philippines. They are incredibly addictive and one is seldom enough. Omit the chicken and prawns if a vegetarian version is preferred.

INGREDIENTS

Spring roll or egg roll wrappers	12–15 pieces
Corn flour (cornstarch)	1 Tbsp, mixed with 2 Tbsp water
Cooking oil	for deep-frying

GARLIC-VINEGAR DIPPING SAUCE

Distilled vinegar	125 ml (4 fl oz / $1/2$ cup)
Water	60 ml (2 fl oz / $1/4$ cup)
Garlic	4 cloves, peeled and lightly crushed
Salt	$1/4$ tsp
Ground black pepper	$1/4$ tsp
Sugar	1 Tbsp
Bird's eye chillies	3, crushed

FILLING

Cooking oil	60 ml (2 fl oz / $1/4$ cup)
Garlic	4 cloves, peeled and chopped
Onion	1, medium, peeled and sliced
Fish sauce	1 Tbsp
Chicken fillet	200 g (7 oz), diced
Prawns (shrimps)	110 g (4 oz), peeled
Water	125 ml (4 fl oz / $1/2$ cup)
Sweet potato	60 g (2 oz), peeled and sliced into strips
French beans	100 g ($3^1/2$ oz), diagonally sliced into strips
Carrot	60 g (2 oz), peeled and sliced into strips
Bean sprouts	200 g (7 oz), tailed, rinsed and drained
Salt	$1/2$ tsp or to taste
Ground white pepper	$1/2$ tsp

METHOD

- Prepare garlic-vinegar dipping sauce. In a saucepan, combine vinegar and water. Without stirring, bring to the boil over medium heat for a few seconds. Remove from heat and leave aside to cool completely. Add remaining ingredients and set aside to cool before serving.

- Prepare filling. In a wok, heat oil over medium heat and fry garlic until golden brown. Add onion and fry until onion is soft and translucent. Add fish sauce and stir to mix well. Add chicken and prawns and fry until they change colour and are cooked.

- Add water, then add sweet potato and fry until slightly tender. Add French beans and carrot and fry for 3 minutes. Add bean sprouts and toss gently to mix well. Season with salt and pepper. Remove from heat and strain filling through a colander to drain excess liquid. Set aside to cool.

- Place a spring roll or egg wrapper on a flat work surface with a corner facing you. Spoon 2–3 Tbsp filling in a line near the corner facing you. Fold in left and right corners over filling, then fold bottom corner over and roll up tightly. Dab with a little corn flour mixture to seal. Repeat with remaining ingredients.

- In a wok, heat oil for deep-frying over medium to high heat. Gently lower in spring rolls and deep-fry until light golden brown. Remove from heat and drain well.

- Serve immediately, with garlic-vinegar dipping sauce on the side.

prawns in garlic sauce (gambas)

Said to originate from the northwest of Spain, *Gambas* is a favourite tapa, or appetiser in the Philippines.

INGREDIENTS

Olive oil	90 ml (3 fl oz / 3/8 cup)
Garlic	1 head, peeled and chopped
Prawns (shrimps)	500 g (1 lb 1 1/2 oz) medium-size, peeled and deveined, with tails left intact
Bird's eye chillies	3, crushed, or use 1 tsp chilli flakes
Tomato paste	1 Tbsp
Paprika	1 tsp
Worcestershire sauce	2 tsp
Dry white wine (optional)	2 Tbsp
Sugar	1 tsp
Salt	1/2 tsp
Ground black pepper	1 1/2 tsp

METHOD

- In a frying pan, heat oil over medium heat and fry garlic until golden brown.

- Add prawns and increase heat to medium-high. Stir-fry until prawns turn pink. Add remaining ingredients and toss to mix well. Remove from heat and set aside.

- If desired, lightly grease a hot plate with a little oil and heat over an open flame. Transfer prawns to hot plate and serve immediately.

salted beef slices (tapa)

This Filipino adaptation of beef jerky is usually served for breakfast in the Philippines, together with Filipino-style Fried Rice (page 37), fried egg and tomato salsa.

INGREDIENTS

Salt	½ Tbsp
White sugar	60 g (2 oz)
Brown sugar	30 g (1 oz)
Beef fillet or sirloin	500 g (1 lb 1½ oz), thinly sliced into 10 × 12-cm (4 × 5-in) slices of 0.2-cm (⅛-in) thickness
Pineapple juice	125 ml (4 fl oz / ½ cup)
Cooking oil	60 ml (2 fl oz / ¼ cup)

NOTE
Before frying, the marinated beef slices can be dried in a windy place for 8 hours, which gives the beef a chewy and crunchy texture.

METHOD

- Prepare a day in advance.
- In a bowl, combine salt and both types of sugar. Add beef slices and marinate them thoroughly by rubbing in the seasoning with fingers.
- Add pineapple juice, cover and refrigerate overnight.
- In a frying pan, heat oil over medium to high heat. Fry beef until light brown and tender.
- Serve immediately on its own or as a side dish with Filipino-style Fried Rice (page 37).

weights and measures

Quantities for this book are given in Metric, Imperial and American (spoon and cup) measures. Standard spoon and cup measurements used are: 1 tsp = 5 ml, 1 Tbsp = 15 ml, 1 cup = 250 ml. All measures are level unless otherwise stated.

Liquid And Volume Measures

Metric	Imperial	American
5 ml	1/6 fl oz	1 teaspoon
10 ml	1/3 fl oz	1 dessertspoon
15 ml	1/2 fl oz	1 tablespoon
60 ml	2 fl oz	1/4 cup (4 tablespoons)
85 ml	2 1/2 fl oz	1/3 cup
90 ml	3 fl oz	3/8 cup (6 tablespoons)
125 ml	4 fl oz	1/2 cup
180 ml	6 fl oz	3/4 cup
250 ml	8 fl oz	1 cup
300 ml	10 fl oz (1/2 pint)	1 1/4 cups
375 ml	12 fl oz	1 1/2 cups
435 ml	14 fl oz	1 3/4 cups
500 ml	16 fl oz	2 cups
625 ml	20 fl oz (1 pint)	2 1/2 cups
750 ml	24 fl oz (1 1/5 pints)	3 cups
1 litre	32 fl oz (1 3/5 pints)	4 cups
1.25 litres	40 fl oz (2 pints)	5 cups
1.5 litres	48 fl oz (2 2/5 pints)	6 cups
2.5 litres	80 fl oz (4 pints)	10 cups

Dry Measures

Metric	Imperial
30 grams	1 ounce
45 grams	1 1/2 ounces
55 grams	2 ounces
70 grams	2 1/2 ounces
85 grams	3 ounces
100 grams	3 1/2 ounces
110 grams	4 ounces
125 grams	4 1/2 ounces
140 grams	5 ounces
280 grams	10 ounces
450 grams	16 ounces (1 pound)
500 grams	1 pound, 1 1/2 ounces
700 grams	1 1/2 pounds
800 grams	1 3/4 pounds
1 kilogram	2 pounds, 3 ounces
1.5 kilograms	3 pounds, 4 1/2 ounces
2 kilograms	4 pounds, 6 ounces

Length

Metric	Imperial
0.5 cm	1/4 inch
1 cm	1/2 inch
1.5 cm	3/4 inch
2.5 cm	1 inch

Oven Temperature

	°C	°F	Gas Regulo
Very slow	120	250	1
Slow	150	300	2
Moderately slow	160	325	3
Moderate	180	350	4
Moderately hot	190/200	375/400	5/6
Hot	210/220	410/425	6/7
Very hot	230	450	8
Super hot	250/290	475/550	9/10

Abbreviation

tsp	teaspoon
Tbsp	tablespoon
g	gram
kg	kilogram
ml	millilitre